AF263694

Sa' Iyda Contee Young

PUTTING MYSELF
FIRST

A Journal & Planner For Every Child to Adolescent Healing From Any Form of Trauma

JOURNAL JOY
An Imprint of Journal Joy Publishers
www.thejournaljoy.com

All rights reserved and printed in the United States of America. No part of this book may be reproduced, distributed, or transmitted in any form or by any means, without the authors' prior written permission, except in the case of brief quotations embodied in critical reviews and specific other noncommercial uses permitted by copyright law.

For Publishing Information, contact Journal Joy at Info@thejournaljoy.com.
www.thejournaljoy.com

Hardcover ISBN: 978-1-957751-74-0
Paperback ISBN: 978-1-957751-75-7
Edited by: Khalia Murray

Dedication

This book is dedicated to my children, grandparents, my parents, and me.
We made it and the trauma did not make us.

You have made a choice to be better for a reason and that reason is **YOU**!

Don't allow yourself to go back to habits and situations that were not helping you to evolve into your full potential.
You must remind yourself daily why you choose to move forward and take the bad with the good and continue to push through and make something great out of yourself. Believing in yourself. No one can take your power and no one can dictate your future.

Trauma can be described in many experiences. They can include the below:

- Bullying
- Loss of a Loved One
- Being Raised in Foster Care
- Abuse, Broken Homes
- Living in A Shelter
- Coping with everyday struggles like College Studies, Daily Homework, Eating Disorder

The goal is to assure that YOU, our youth; are NOT alone and love and support is all that is needed. With determination and the strength to push through; in addition to the knowledge and tools to know anything and everything, anything is obtainable and your dreams are reachable by simply not giving up.

This Journal Belongs To:

____

Yearly Plan

YEAR : 2024

JANUARY

- Create a vision board
- Develop a monthly budget
- Enroll in any courses
- Start a daily journal
- Reflect on achievements
- Specific goals for the year

FEBRUARY

- Establish a daily routine
- Identify any bad habits
- Obstacles that hinder your progress and begin addressing them
- Connect with mentors

MARCH

- Update goals based on progress
- evolving aspirations
- Prioritize self-care activities
- Seek feedback from peers

APRIL

- Explore potential collaborations
- Start building an online presence
- Personal brand through social media

MAY

- Conduct a thorough review of current skill
- Identify areas for improvement
- Create a learning plan that includes books, podcasts, or online courses

JUNE

- Attend conferences, webinars, or workshops relevant field
- Volunteer or engage in community service to give back and broaden your perspective

JULY

- Begin tracking key performance indicators
- Join relevant online communities to expand professional network
- Begin working on a long-term project

AUGUST

- Evaluate and streamline daily routines
- Processes for increased efficiency
- Set short-term milestones to stay motivated and maintain momentum

SEPTEMEBER

- Seek out opportunities to present
- Speak at industry events or local gatherings
- Develop a mentorship relationship or offer mentorship

OCTOBER

- Conduct a SWOT analysis
- Dedicate time for reflection
- Celebrate accomplishments from the first half of the year
- Identify any areas

NOVEMBER

- Engage in networking activities to forge new connections
- Explore potential collaborations
- Identify and implement new tools

DECEMBER

- Evaluate your budget and make any necessary adjustments
- Set aside time for personal development
- Take a vacation or plan a break to recharge

Table of Contents:

Who Am I?

I Am Amazing!

30-day challenge

NEW HABIT:

Why it matters:

I Did Great!

I'll try again:

My Gift to Myself:

I can do this!

How did it go?

What did I learn?

HOW DOES IT FEEL? ☆☆☆☆☆

JOURNAL ENTRY DATE:

GIVE YOURSELF A COMPLIMENT.

HOW WILL YOU MAKE SOMEONE SMILE TODAY?

WHAT CAN YOU ACCOMPLISH TODAY?

MONTHLY PLANNER

MON	TUE	WED	THU	FRI	SAT	SUN

TO DO

DATE

SPECIAL DATES

NOTES

NOTES

NOTES

NOTES

NOTES

My Story

**There's Nothing I Can't Do
If I Set My Mind To It!**

30-day challenge

NEW HABIT:

Why it matters:

I Did Great!

I'll try again:

My Gift to Myself:

I can do this!

How did it go?

What did I learn?

HOW DOES IT FEEL? ☆☆☆☆☆

JOURNAL ENTRY DATE:

GIVE YOURSELF A COMPLIMENT.

HOW WILL YOU MAKE SOMEONE SMILE TODAY?

WHAT CAN YOU ACCOMPLISH TODAY?

MONTHLY PLANNER

MON	TUE	WED	THU	FRI	SAT	SUN

TO DO **DATE** **SPECIAL DATES**

NOTES

NOTES

NOTES

NOTES

NOTES

My Happiest Moments

You Are Worthy!

30-day challenge

NEW HABIT:

Why it matters:

I Did Great!

I'll try again:

My Gift to Myself:

I can do this!

How did it go?

What did I learn?

HOW DOES IT FEEL?

GIVE YOURSELF A COMPLIMENT.

HOW WILL YOU MAKE SOMEONE SMILE TODAY?

WHAT CAN YOU ACCOMPLISH TODAY?

MONTHLY PLANNER

MON	TUE	WED	THU	FRI	SAT	SUN

TO DO

DATE

SPECIAL DATES

NOTES

NOTES

NOTES

NOTES

NOTES

Self Forgiveness

I Must Put Myself First!

30-day challenge

NEW HABIT:

Why it matters:

I Did Great!

I'll try again:

My Gift to Myself:

I can do this!

How did it go?

What did I learn?

HOW DOES IT FEEL?

JOURNAL ENTRY DATE:

GIVE YOURSELF A COMPLIMENT.

HOW WILL YOU MAKE SOMEONE SMILE TODAY?

WHAT CAN YOU ACCOMPLISH TODAY?

MONTHLY PLANNER

MON	TUE	WED	THU	FRI	SAT	SUN

TO DO   **DATE**

SPECIAL DATES

NOTES

NOTES

NOTES

NOTES

NOTES

Look at my Inner Circle

I Am In Competition With Myself!

30-day challenge

NEW HABIT:

Why it matters:

I Did Great!

I'll try again:

My Gift to Myself:

I can do this!

How did it go?

What did I learn?

HOW DOES IT FEEL? ☆☆☆☆☆

JOURNAL ENTRY DATE:

GIVE YOURSELF A COMPLIMENT.

HOW WILL YOU MAKE SOMEONE SMILE TODAY?

WHAT CAN YOU ACCOMPLISH TODAY?

MONTHLY PLANNER

MON	TUE	WED	THU	FRI	SAT	SUN

TO DO	DATE	SPECIAL DATES

NOTES

NOTES

NOTES

NOTES

NOTES

Self Improvement Mentally

I Am Good Enough!

30-day challenge

NEW HABIT:

Why it matters:

I Did Great!

I'll try again:

My Gift to Myself:

I can do this!

How did it go?

What did I learn?

HOW DOES IT FEEL? ☆☆☆☆☆

JOURNAL ENTRY DATE:

GIVE YOURSELF A COMPLIMENT.

HOW WILL YOU MAKE SOMEONE SMILE TODAY?

WHAT CAN YOU ACCOMPLISH TODAY?

MONTHLY PLANNER

MON	TUE	WED	THU	FRI	SAT	SUN

TO DO

DATE

SPECIAL DATES

NOTES

NOTES

NOTES

NOTES

NOTES

NOTES

Self Improvement - Physical

**Its Okay To Fail
But It's Not Okay To Give Up!**

30-day challenge

NEW HABIT:

Why it matters:

I Did Great!

I'll try again:

My Gift to Myself:

I can do this!

How did it go?

What did I learn?

HOW DOES IT FEEL? ☆ ☆ ☆ ☆ ☆

JOURNAL ENTRY DATE:

GIVE YOURSELF A COMPLIMENT.

HOW WILL YOU MAKE SOMEONE SMILE TODAY?

WHAT CAN YOU ACCOMPLISH TODAY?

MONTHLY PLANNER

| MON | TUE | WED | THU | FRI | SAT | SUN |

TO DO

DATE

SPECIAL DATES

NOTES

NOTES

NOTES

NOTES

NOTES

Where Do I See Myself in 5-10 Years

Go Out And Get It!

30-day challenge

NEW HABIT: _______________________________

Why it matters: ___________________________

____

I Did Great! ______________________________

I'll try again: ____________________________

My Gift to Myself: _________________________

I can do this!

How did it go? ____________________________

____

What did I learn? _________________________

____

HOW DOES IT FEEL? ☆☆☆☆☆

JOURNAL ENTRY DATE:

GIVE YOURSELF A COMPLIMENT.

HOW WILL YOU MAKE SOMEONE SMILE TODAY?

WHAT CAN YOU ACCOMPLISH TODAY?

MONTHLY PLANNER

MON	TUE	WED	THU	FRI	SAT	SUN

TO DO

DATE

SPECIAL DATES

NOTES

NOTES

NOTES

NOTES

NOTES

Social Media Can Help Me

I Love Myself!

30-day challenge

NEW HABIT:

Why it matters:

I Did Great!

I'll try again:

My Gift to Myself:

I can do this!

How did it go?

What did I learn?

HOW DOES IT FEEL? ☆☆☆☆☆

GIVE YOURSELF A COMPLIMENT.

HOW WILL YOU MAKE SOMEONE SMILE TODAY?

WHAT CAN YOU ACCOMPLISH TODAY?

MONTHLY PLANNER

MON	TUE	WED	THU	FRI	SAT	SUN

TO DO | DATE

SPECIAL DATES

NOTES

NOTES

NOTES

NOTES

NOTES

What Resources Will Keep in My Back Pocket

Nobody will Love Me
As Good As I Love Myself!

30-day challenge

NEW HABIT:

Why it matters:

I Did Great!

I'll try again:

My Gift to Myself:

I can do this!

How did it go?

What did I learn?

HOW DOES IT FEEL?   ☆☆☆☆☆

JOURNAL ENTRY DATE:

GIVE YOURSELF A COMPLIMENT.

HOW WILL YOU MAKE SOMEONE SMILE TODAY?

WHAT CAN YOU ACCOMPLISH TODAY?

MONTHLY PLANNER

MON	TUE	WED	THU	FRI	SAT	SUN

TO DO	DATE	SPECIAL DATES

NOTES

NOTES

NOTES

NOTES

NOTES

Losing Is Not In My Vocabulary!

30-day challenge

NEW HABIT:

Why it matters:

I Did Great!

I'll try again:

My Gift to Myself:

I can do this!

How did it go?

What did I learn?

HOW DOES IT FEEL?

JOURNAL ENTRY DATE:

GIVE YOURSELF A COMPLIMENT.

HOW WILL YOU MAKE SOMEONE SMILE TODAY?

WHAT CAN YOU ACCOMPLISH TODAY?

MONTHLY PLANNER

MON	TUE	WED	THU	FRI	SAT	SUN

TO DO   DATE   SPECIAL DATES

NOTES

NOTES

NOTES

NOTES

NOTES

Take a Walk. Fresh Air
Is Important!

SMILE :)

YOU ARE IMPORTANT!

KISS YOURSELF TODAY :)

Naps are so good :)

YOUR WANTS MATTER!

YOU MATTER!

Asking for help is
OK.

JOURNAL ENTRY DATE:

GIVE YOURSELF A COMPLIMENT.

HOW WILL YOU MAKE SOMEONE SMILE TODAY?

WHAT CAN YOU ACCOMPLISH TODAY?

Your mental health matters

SYMPTOMS OF ANXIETY

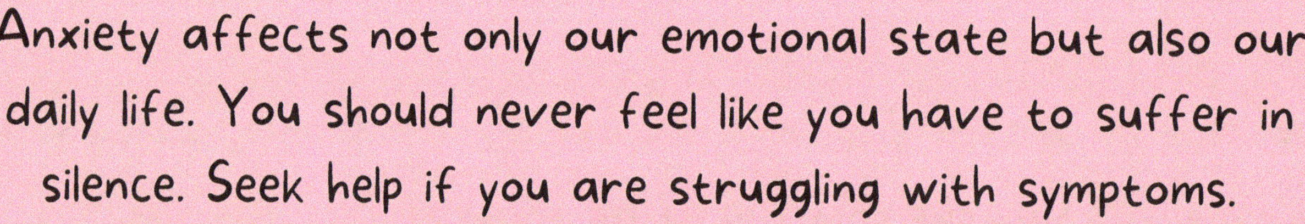

Anxiety affects not only our emotional state but also our daily life. You should never feel like you have to suffer in silence. Seek help if you are struggling with symptoms.

1 Insert first symptom

2 Insert first symptom

3 Insert first symptom

4 Insert first symptom

5 Insert first symptom

6 Insert first symptom

For more information, please visit:
www.reallygreatsite.com

NOTES

NOTES

NOTES

NOTES

NOTES

JOURNAL ENTRY DATE:

GIVE YOURSELF A COMPLIMENT.

HOW WILL YOU MAKE SOMEONE SMILE TODAY?

WHAT CAN YOU ACCOMPLISH TODAY?

NOTES

NOTES

NOTES

NOTES

NOTES

Sometimes It's Just A Bad Day, Not A Bad Life

It's Okay To Not Feel Okay Today.

JOURNAL ENTRY DATE:

GIVE YOURSELF A COMPLIMENT.

HOW WILL YOU MAKE SOMEONE SMILE TODAY?

WHAT CAN YOU ACCOMPLISH TODAY?

NOTES

NOTES

NOTES

NOTES

NOTES

WORKOUT DAY GOALS!

START!

FINISH !

YOU CAN DO IT!!

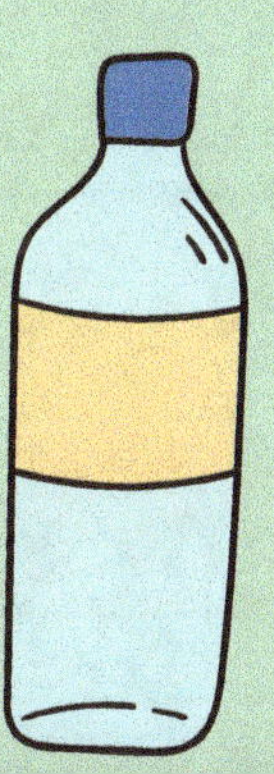

JOURNAL ENTRY DATE:

GIVE YOURSELF A COMPLIMENT.

HOW WILL YOU MAKE SOMEONE SMILE TODAY?

WHAT CAN YOU ACCOMPLISH TODAY?

SLEEP HYGIENE

FIVE EFFECTIVE TIPS TO ESTABLISH A HEALTHY SLEEPING

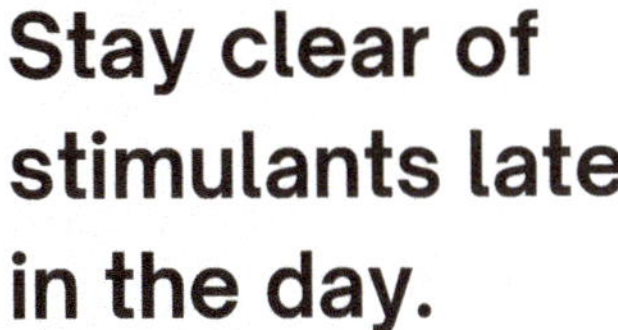

Stay clear of stimulants late in the day.

avoid beverages and foods that contain caffeine

Do a regular exercise.

regular exercise routine can help contribute to improved sleep.

Create a relaxing bedtime/pre-bedtime routine.

any relaxing activity about an hour before bed helps creates a smoother transition.

Stick to a consistent sleep schedule.

going to bed and waking up at the same time every day

Unplug an hour before bed.

Keep screen use to a minimum, at least an hour before bed,

Keep your room cool and comfortable.

ideal room for sleeping is cool, quiet, and dark.

Avoid foods that can disrupt sleep.

when you lie down right after a big meal, your digestive juices are still cranking.

JOURNAL ENTRY DATE:

GIVE YOURSELF A COMPLIMENT.

HOW WILL YOU MAKE SOMEONE SMILE TODAY?

WHAT CAN YOU ACCOMPLISH TODAY?

World MENTAL HEALTH *Day*

TAKE CARE OF YOURSELF

CONTACT US

www.jamailasmentalhealth.com

MOVIE REVIEW

Title:

Director:

Rate the movie: 

What is your favorite scene in the movie?

____

____

Draw your favorite character from the movie and describe him or her in 1-2 sentences.

____

____

____

IT'S OKAY TO ASK FOR HELP
YOU DON'T HAVE TO FIGHT YOUR BATTLE ALONE. TALK TO US.
WWW.JAMAILASMENTALHEALTH.COM

DAILY MEAL PLANNER

Date:

Breakfast	Lunch

Dinner	Snack

Shopping List:

Weekly Planner

Monday

Tuesday

Wednesday

Thursday

Friday

Saturday

Sunday

NOTES

NOTES

NOTES

NOTES

NOTES

TIME TO TRAVEL!

TO-DO LIST

REMEMBER

NOTES

WEEKLY MEAL PLAN

Date:

Day	Meal	Water Intake
Sun		
Mon		
Tue		
Wed		
Thu		
Fri		
Sat		

NOTES

NOTES

NOTES

NOTES

NOTES

MOVIE REVIEW

Title:

Director:

Rate the movie: 

What is your favorite scene in the movie?

____

____

Draw your favorite character from the movie and describe him or her in 1-2 sentences.

____

____

____

weekend to-do list

52 WEEKS SAVINGS

WEEK	DEPOSIT	BALANCE	DONE	WEEK	DEPOSIT	BALANCE	DONE
1				27			
2				28			
3				29			
4				30			
5				31			
6				32			
7				33			
8				34			
9				35			
10				36			
11				37			
12				38			
13				39			
14				40			
15				41			
16				42			
17				43			
18				44			
19				45			
20				46			
21				47			
22				48			
23				49			
24				50			
25				51			
26				52			

MONTHLY SAVINGS TRACKER

MONTH:

DATE	DESCRIPTION	DEPOSIT	WITHDRAWAL	BALANCE

TOTAL	

NOTES

NOTES

NOTES

NOTES

NOTES

NOTES

NOTES

Trust that you will make it.
Everything will be okay.
Never give up on your Dreams and Goals.
You have to find peace with yourself in order to have peace with others.
Being grateful for every day is a chance to be better than yesterday.
Learn from your mistakes and the mistakes of others.
If you believe it, you can achieve it!
Your path will get clear just stay consistent with yourself.
You will make it through.
Create new paths to clear out the old.
Think bigger. Dream bigger!
Be willing to listen and learn.
Welcome new beginnings.
Live life, and create new memories.

Drugs won't heal my pain.

10 Ways
to Start Building Healthy Habits

Seek professional help if you feel like you need assistance.

Get adequate sleep every night.

Persevere when you face setbacks.

Incorporate physical activity into your routine.

Make time for activities that make you happy

Eat healthy foods and limit your intake of junk food

Spend time with positive people who support your healthy lifestyle.

Set realistic goals for and strive to accomplish them.

Avoid smoking and excessive alcohol consumption.

Practice stress-relieving techniques.

About The Author:

Sa'lyda Contee Young and her family have experienced trauma. Their family was torn apart by incarceration. The trauma they endured was extremely difficult as a family with young adult children. Sa'lyda was able to face her trauma and stay dedicated to focusing on her children and their needs as well as herself.

Today Sa'lyda is an accomplished business owner and consultant assisting Fortune 500 Hundred Companies.

Her two children both have graduated from high school, and college, and are now pursuing advanced college degrees with their future in medical and design professions.

Learn more about Sa"lyda and Jamaila's Heath Group at: **www.jamailasmentalhealth.com**

www.ingramcontent.com/pod-product-compliance
Lightning Source LLC
Chambersburg PA
CBHW081301090726
47818CB00080B/208